THE AWARDS

THE ASSOCIATION OF PHOTOGRAPHERS TWELFTH AWARDS 1995

We would like to thank the following who have helped us with their time and effort, and
the members of The Association of Photographers whose support makes The Awards possible.

THE JUDGES

TONY BOWRAN	MICK DEAN
VINCE FROST	MARTIN GALTON
DERRICK HASS	GRAHAM HENDERSON
WENDY HINTON	DAVID HISCOCK
GARY MARTIN	TIM MOTION
RAY MASSEY	PETER MYERS
ARTHUR PARSONS	DAVID PEARCE
MARK REDDY	TOM STODDART
AIDAN SULLIVAN	

THE ORGANISERS

SUE ALLAT	JACKIE KELLEY
VALERIE MAY	JAY MYRDAL
ANDREW OLNEY	NIGEL PARRY
ALEX STEELE-MORTIMER	

ALSO: Gwen Thomas, Mike Laye and Optikos

TYPESETTING AND ARTWORK: The Saward Roberts Studio
Telephone: 0171-336 7480
FRONT COVER PHOTOGRAPH: Tony May

The Association of Photographers, 9-10 Domingo Street, London EC1Y 0TA, England
Telephone: 0171-608 1441 Fax: 0171-253 3007

Published by Reed Information Services, Windsor Court, East Grinstead House,
East Grinstead, West Sussex RH19 1XA, England. Telephone: 01342 326972

Printed and bound in China
Produced by Mandarin Offset Limited

ISBN 0 611 00849 1

C reative inspiration is one of those strange intangible processes - a rare and precious moment in time.

Subjective judgement of this creativity, reflected in the Twelfth Awards Book, again provides us with another example of British photography at its best.

Congratulations to all members who participated in The Awards this year, to those shown in the following pages, this is your moment - enjoy it.

The Association of Photographers Twelfth Awards

The book sponsored and published by the Creative Handbook

RICHARD WOOLLEY

Publisher

THE
CREATIVE
HAND
BOOK
1995

Published by the Media Division of Reed Information Services

A member of the Reed Elsevier Plc Group

PHOTOGRAPH OF MARTIN BECKETT BY MIKE LAYE
Electronically retouched by Optikos Laboratories (part of the Adplates Group)

The Association is here to create an environment in which creative photography can thrive and The Awards are obviously the very sharp end of this movement. They provide an insight both into the recent past and the future, allowing a faster and easier track for users of photography to push creative boundaries ever forward and maintain British photography's high international status.

This highly successful environment, however, cannot exist unless we also maintain and improve the respect for photographers' rights which form the very basis from which our community's strength springs. Mutual respect, not exploitation, is required to produce truly challenging work and the pictures contained within this book should inspire us all to work towards a situation where such creativity will continue to thrive.

MARTIN BECKETT

Chairman of The Association of Photographers

PHOTOGRAPH OF THE TWELFTH AWARDS COMMITTEE BY MIKE LAYE
Electronically retouched by Optikos Laboratories (part of the Adplates Group)
Front row left to right: Jay Myrdal, Valerie May, Nigel Parry
Back row left to right: Alex Steele-Mortimer, Andrew Olney, Sue Allatt, Jackie Kelley

T wo thousand four hundred images were entered into The Twelfth Awards, up by twenty seven percent on last year. Fortunately, by adding an extra half day for the briefing and preview, the judges had two and a half days in total to make the final selection for the book; which is just as well because without this and our efficient computer based judging system, it is unlikely we could have managed the task.

"You can please all of the people some of the time ..."

With an average pass rate of only seven percent there are, of course, many fine images which do not make the final selection and with this in mind we have added a new and no doubt controversial category. Called 'Judges' Choice', it is an opportunity for each judge to unilaterally rescue a favourite image which would not otherwise be selected. A very interesting addition to the book this year.

The Awards are not a static entity but have grown and developed over the years. The bulk of the work is done by our staff committee members, but photographer members are an essential part of the formula. The importance of The Awards is such that few photographers can afford to serve on the committee long, standing down in order to enter work themselves. For these reasons we will always need new people to help pilot The Awards into the future. Under their guidance The Awards will continue to develop as we react to the changes the new technologies are bringing to our industry.

JAY MYRDAL
Chairman of the Awards Committee

The Association of Photographers was first launched in 1968 and is a non-profit making trade association for professional photographers. Our principal aims are to protect and improve the rights of fashion, advertising and editorial photographers and to promote the highest standards of work and business practices throughout the industry. Over the years, by encouraging continuous discussion and development of all aspects of the profession, we have made significant and dramatic improvements for our members.

The premises in Domingo Street are the centre for all The Association's activities and include our own library and gallery. The Association Gallery provides a varied and exciting exhibition programme promoting our members' work. From these headquarters we also publish our monthly magazine IMAGE, which is a well respected information source and opinion leader. Our services include a wide-ranging computerised information system to aid our members, a freelance assistant service, careers talks and Job Board, workshops, plus an education and training department, which plays a significant role in promoting, maintaining and developing relationships between all levels of higher and further education and the professional photographic industry. Legal services are also available to members and The Association continues to play an integral part in developmental projects dealing with rights, ethics and standards of practise of professional photographers in the UK and Europe.

W ithout the generosity and continued support of our sponsors and members, The Awards would not have continued to progress each successive year to the high status they have now acquired. By creating a forum for discussion and consideration The Awards have created an excellent vehicle for The Association to demonstrate the quality of its members personal and commissioned work to the world at large.

The Awards Book is now recognised within the photographic industry as one of the best references of current photography from professional photographers. The books, which have become collectors' items, now grace the shelves of the most discerning people. The Awards, which are only open to members of The Association of Photographers encourage new personal work to be produced, which can be seen on the following pages along side top commissioned images.

The judges assessing The Awards are all experts in their respective fields and the Awards Committee are confident that their collective knowledge has resulted in a balanced judgement. We congratulate everyone who has been selected for this book and hope that you too, will gain enjoyment from its pages.

PHOTOGRAPH OF THE JUDGES BY MIKE LAYE
Electronically retouched by Optikos Laboratories (part of the Adplates Group)

TONY BOWRAN – Photographer

Tony Bowran covers a variety of advertising work, from table top to large sets and cars, as well as personal work projects. He has won a Gold, two Silver and two Merit Awards in the non-commissioned sections. Tony graduated from the L.C.P. in 1976 and is an épée fencer with a current GB ranking.

MICK DEAN – Photographer

Mick Dean's main areas of work are food and still life. Mick also shoots TV commercials. He is a founding member of The Association of Photographers (then AFAEP) and worked on various committees for 10 years. Mick started the 'education' section and put it on the road!

VINCE FROST – Art Director/Designer

Vince Frost is art director/designer of BIG Magazine, as well as working on album design, book covers, posters and corporate ID. Vince was the youngest associate partner at Pentogram Design, which he joined in 1989. He left just over a year ago and set up Frost Design, where one of his main projects is BIG, a large format Spanish/English 'life' magazine for designers, photographers and the fashion industry. BIG magazine has been nominated for Best Designed publication D&AD 1994.

MARTIN GALTON – Head of Art, Leagus Delaney

Martin Galton recently became Head of Art at Leagus Delaney having previously spent 8 years at Bartle Bogle Hegarty. He is happiest when sploshing oils around a canvas and he recently attended a course at an art school in Tunbridge Wells where he held his first one man show. There were so many complaints from the locals that they were forced to close the course down!

DERRICK HASS – Art Director, McCann Erickson

Derrick Hass is an Art Director at McCann Erickson. He is engaged in creating TV commercials, press ads and posters. Derrick has worked at CDP, BMP, Saatchi & Saatchi and many other agencies in his long career. His work has been selected for the archives of The Victoria and Albert Museum and The Royal College of Art. Derrick has also won 7 D&AD pencils and numerous other awards, including Gold and Silver Lions and many Campaign Press and Poster Award Silvers, as well as Gold and Silver Arrows at the British Television Awards.

GRAHAM HENDERSON – Photographer

Graham Henderson specialises in roomsets and interiors.

WENDY HINTON – Picture Editor, ES Magazine

Wendy Hinton has been commissioning photography for ES Magazine since its launch in 1987. As well as using established photographers she is keen to encourage and commission new talent. Wendy is married with a three year old daughter.

DAVID HISCOCK – Photographer

David Hiscock's main areas of work comprise exhibiting and teaching, while his commercial work includes many areas covering advertising, fashion and portraits. David's major commissions have included English and German Vogue, Virgin Records, Singapore Airlines and Carlsberg Lager. He has won numerous photographic awards and exhibited in a large number of one-man and group exhibitions throughout the world. David was chosen to be the British Olympic artist at the Barcelona Olympic Games.

GARY MARTIN – Art Director, Bartle Bogle Hegarty

Gary Martin is an art director at Bartle Bogle Hegarty where his main areas of work include posters, press and television. He has won three D&AD Silvers, two D&AD Silver Nominations and two Campaign Poster Golds – for Nike, the Terrence Higgins Trust and Pepsi. Gary enjoyed judging the Twelfth Awards very much, but never wants to see another photograph of a rusty farm implement again.

FRONT ROW LEFT TO RIGHT: TIM MOTION, DAVID HISCOCK, MICK DEAN
BACK ROW LEFT TO RIGHT: TONY BOWRAN, PETER MYERS, RAY MASSEY, GRAHAM HENDERSON, TOM STODDART

PHOTOGRAPH OF THE JUDGES BY MIKE LAYE
Electronically retouched by Optikos Laboratories (part of the Adplates Group)

RAY MASSEY – Photographer
Ray Massey works mainly in advertising, still life and people photography. Ray is also well known for manipulative work in effects and production. He says that his 'Claims to Fame' are not numerous enough to mention!

TIM MOTION – Photographer
Tim Motion is a Gold Award winner, specialising in location, architecture and aerial photography. He is currently working on a book featuring blues and jazz musicians.

PETER MYERS – Photographer
Peter Myers is an advertising photographer specialising in still life and food.

ARTHUR PARSONS – Senior Art Director and Associate Director, CDP, now retired
Arthur Parsons was a founder member of CDP in 1960, and remained there throughout his career. He has worked with many of the top photographers in this country and in the States. Arthur has won numerous D&AD, Creative Circle and London TV awards, which also included D&AD Gold and Silver awards for 'Army Officer Recruiting' and 'Metropolitan Police' campaigns. In 1979 Arthur was made President of D&AD (the first advertising art director to be made President). Arthur presented the Eleventh Awards for The Association of Photographers in 1994, and now spends most of his time in the studio painting. He has had work accepted by the Institute of Painters in Watercolour, and is represented by two London galleries.

DAVID PEARCE – Design Director, Tatham Pearce
As Design Director at Tatham Pearce, David Pearce works on the design and preparation of all forms of corporate communications, including annual reports, company and product brochures, and corporate identities. David started his career as designer/photographer before joining Pentagram as a Senior Designer. Since 1978 he has run his own consultancies, forming Tatham Pearce seven years ago. David's major clients include Lloyds Bank, Barclays Bank and MFI. He was responsible for Land Rover's up-dated corporate identity and was a member of a core team responsible for the launch of Discovery and the new Range Rover, designing product brochures for both vehicles. David regularly commissions and art directs photography for all forms of design requirements. David Pearce has been a member of D&AD since 1974, and is a Fellow of the Chartered Society of Designers.

MARK REDDY – Creative Group Head, Saatchi & Saatchi
Mark Reddy is Creative Group Head at Saatchi & Saatchi. He has previously worked at Doyle Dane Bernbach and BMP DDB Needham, where he was Head of Art at both advertising agencies. Mark currently works within all areas of advertising, illustration, painting, sculpture and gardening. He has been the winner of D&AD Silvers, Campaign Press Gold and Silvers and Creative Circle Golds. Mark believes passionately in young British photographers and loathes art directors who fly to New York at the drop of a hat!

TOM STODDART – Editorial Photographer
Tom Stoddart is an editorial photographer working on international news events, features and documentary photography. Tom won the Nikon Photographer of the Year in 1990 and 1991, and also gained the World Press Awards in 1992 and 1993. The events Tom covered during 1994 included: Rwanda, Arafat's homecoming to Gaza and the Mandela election.

AIDAN SULLIVAN – Assistant Editor, Sunday Times
Aidan Sullivan is Assistant Editor for the Sunday Times, where, for the past 6 years, he has commissioned photography for the magazine. He has also produced a book called 'War in the Gulf', which is a photographic record of the Gulf War. Aidan is a Trustee of the Ian Parry Memorial Fund.

FRONT ROW LEFT TO RIGHT: VINCE FROST, MARK REDDY, ARTHUR PARSONS
BACK ROW LEFT TO RIGHT: MARK GALTON, GARY MARTIN, DAVID PEARCE, DERRICK HASS, AIDAN SULLIVAN, WENDY HINTON

At a time when there is an array of awards for photographers, The Association Awards are still regarded as the foremost guide to quality within the industry.

Fuji Professional is proud to sponsor The Awards again this year, to continue with its student support and to underline the high value it puts on creativity through Fuji Art.

We are also delighted to continue our sponsorship of the Assistants' Awards, combined with the production this year of a catalogue of images from the exhibition.

Investing in the future of the industry means investing in young photographers and Fuji Professional took on the rewarding job of sponsoring The Association's Job Board and Job Line, together with the Careers Service last year.

Investment in technology is, of course, the life blood of photography and, as one of the world's leading imaging innovators, Fuji Professional is able to support The Association and its Members with its renowned range of products and services.

GRAHAM RUTHERFORD

Divisional Manager

Fuji Professional Photographic Division

Sponsored by

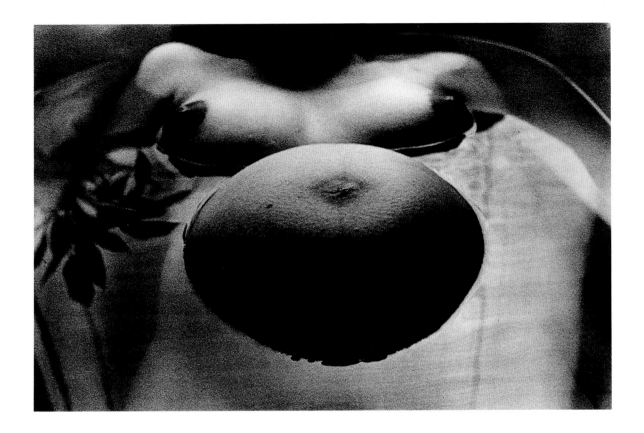

GOLD

Photographer: TONY MAY
Printer: Ron Bagley
Art Director: Tony May

Photographer: RICHARD CLARK
Printer: Richard Clark

MERIT

Photographer: JAMES WORMSER
Printer: Bill Rowlinson
Freckles

Photographer: DEAN STEADMAN
Printer: Dean Steadman
Mask I

Photographer: DEAN STEADMAN
Printer: Dean Steadman
Mask II

MERIT

Photographer: DAVID TACK
Printer: Master Mono
Art Director: David Tack
Teapot Lady, Saigon

Photographer: PHIL HUNT
Printer: Ken Ashby – Master Mono
Forgotten Heroes

Photographer: ADAM HINTON
Printer: Gary Wilson
Family having a picnic on
New Year's Day 1993,
Donetsk, Ukraine

Photographer: GRAHAM WESTMORELAND
Printer: Jean Lock – Visions
The Masaii, The Masaii Marra, Kenya

Agfa is the leading manufacturer of photographic materials in Europe today and provides a whole range of products from quality films, papers and chemicals through to photographic equipment.

Designed with the discerning photographer in mind, the company's products are endorsed by many of the world's top professionals.

Multicontrast Classic is an unsurpassed variable contrast, fibre-based black and white paper which enables printers to obtain subtle image tones that could traditionally only be achieved with Agfa's highly acclaimed exhibition papers, such as Record Rapid.

1994 witnessed the launch of Optima 400 – the ultimate professional film with excellent colour rendition and high colour saturation, available in all popular professional formats.

Agfa is totally dedicated to the professional market which means that photographers and printers alike can always rely on quality for state-of-the-art imaging materials. Materials which are constantly being improved to suit the demands of today's professional.

AGFA

Sponsored by

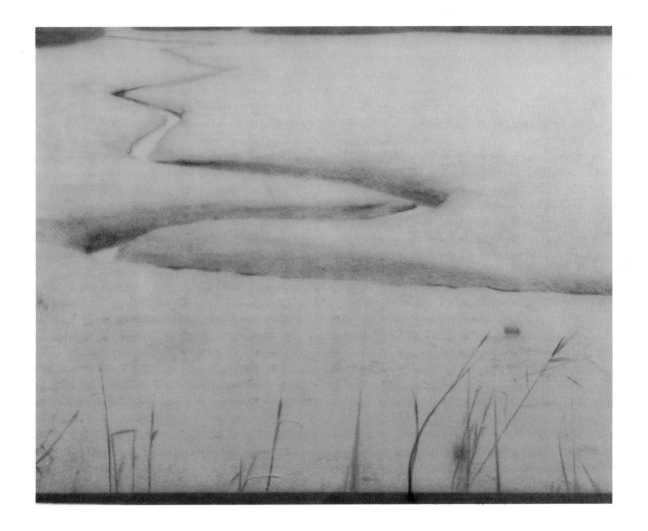

SILVER

Photographer: JUSTIN PUMFREY
Printer: Justin Pumfrey
Snape, Suffolk

MERIT

Photographer: PETE SEAWARD
Printer: Pete Seaward
Tuscany

MERIT

Photographer: DAVID TACK
Printer: Master Mono
Burmese family going to market.
Inlay Lake, Burma

Photographer: DENNIS LEE
Printer: Bill Rowlinson
Bratislava

Photographer: MARTIN BECKETT
Printer: Martin Beckett
Desert Huts

Photographer: PETE SEAWARD
Printer: Pete Seaward
Inverary

Photographer: DOUG CURRIE
Printer: Jean Lock – Visions
Alentejo

Photographer: PEER LINDGREEN
Printer: Peer Lindgreen

Photographer: MEL ALLEN
Printer: Chris – Photographic Techniques
Greece

Photographer: CHRIS LEWIS
Printer: Bill Rowlinson
Crosfield-Mamba: Nick Strong – VBF A'dam
London 94

Photographer: MARTIN BECKETT
Printer: Keith Taylor – Metro
Pueblo

Now in its twelfth year these awards go from strength to strength, as does the commitment and unstinting hard work of The Association of Photographers.

This year, more than ever, our industry has progressed into the field of Electronic Imaging, Joe's Basement being no exception. But our duty also lies in providing the high standard of traditional photographic services you have come to expect from us.

I believe that the coming year will bring to the forefront the creative skills and talent within our industry, with even more innovative and inspirational ideas from members of The Association.

Once again I would like to congratulate all those who have taken part in these awards.

GREGG FORTE
Managing Director
Joe's Basement Limited

Sponsored by

PHOTOGRAPHIC
services

Photographer: CARL WARNER
Printer: Ken Ashby – Master Mono
Dummy

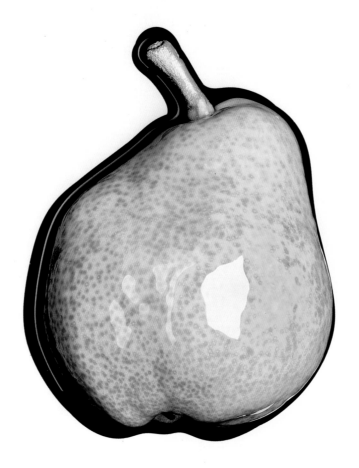

Photographer: TIM WINDSOR
Printer: Cascade

Photographer: PAUL BUSSELL
Printer: Jean Lock – Visions
Peaches

Photographer: TIM WINDSOR
Printer: Cascade

Photographer: GARRY STEVENSON
Printer: Adrian Ensor

I t is, as always, a pleasure to support The Awards.

This year has seen an enormous change for Metro. Firstly, our name has changed, reflecting our growing spread of services, and secondly we moved into a new purpose-built building in EC1. The move brought all of Metro's services under one roof in expanded facilities, with electronic imaging now playing a vital role in the company's service profile.

As the major development in photography in recent years, we are confident that the use of electronic imaging techniques will continue the development of photography as a creative and vital art form, having a profound effect on the type and range of imagery produced.

We whole-heartedly support the enthusiasm and technical excellence illustrated on the following pages, and will continue to be dedicated to supporting the art of the photographer.

BEN RICHARDSON
Managing Director
Metro Imaging Ltd

Sponsored by

METRO

Photographer: MICHAEL DUNNING
Printer: Mike Davis – Metro
Art Director: Michael Dunning
System Operator: Michael Dunning
Wall Street 3-Card Trick

MERIT

Photographer: ANDREW THOMAS
Printer: Ken Grant – Colorific
System Operator: Andrew Thomas
System: Dicomed Imaginator Sport
Digital Laboratory: Electric Pictures

MERIT

Photographer: GILES REVELL
Printer: John Bettell
Mechanical Fish

Photographer: MICHAEL DUNNING
Printer: Mike Davis – Metro
Art Director: Michael Dunning
System Operator: Michael Dunning

Photographer:	FRANK HERHOLDT
Printer:	Mike Davis – Metro
System Operator:	Gandee – Metro
	From Africa

Sky Photographic are proud of our association with The Twelfth Awards and are delighted to be supporting them.

Sky Photographic have for 27 years recognised the essential role of promoting the individual creativity of photographers. Supporting these Awards gives us the platform for continuing this important commitment, and a medium which allows us to say 'Thank You' for your patronage.

We congratulate all who have entered and ensured that the standards remain very high.

ED DAVIES
Marketing and Advertising Manager
Sky Photographic

Sponsored by

SKY
Photographic Services Ltd.

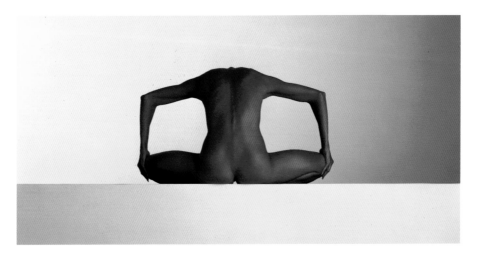

Photographer: SIMON SOMERVILLE
Printer: Peter Young

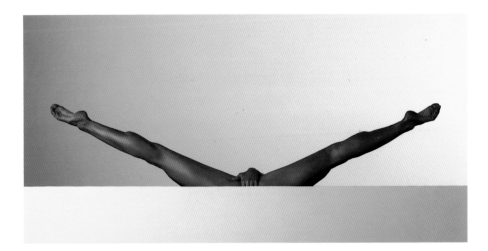

Photographer: SIMON SOMERVILLE
Printer: Peter Young

Photographer: JULIE FISHER
Printer: Direct Colour
Max

SILVER

Photographer: JULIE FISHER
Printer: Direct Colour
         Max

MERIT

Photographer:	MALCOLM VENVILLE
Printer:	Jeff Laine – Wace
Model:	Mark Denton
System Operator:	Tom Finnane – Wace
Hair & Make-up:	Julie Dartnell
Costume:	Jane Field
	Shufflebottom's Guide

MERIT

Photographer: MALCOLM VENVILLE
Printer: Jeff Laine – Wace
Model: Mark Denton
System Operator: Tom Finnane – Wace
Hair & Make-up: Julie Dartnell
Costume: Jane Field
Shufflebottom's Guide

Photographer: ANDREAS HEUMANN
Printer: Jean Lock – Visions (left)
Jean Lock/Andreas Heumann (right)
Tree in Wall, India (left)
Architect's Dream, India (right)

Photographer: ANDREAS HEUMANN
Printer: Jean Lock/Andreas Heumann (top)
Jean Lock – Visions (bottom)
School Outing, India (top)
Relaxed in Taj, India (bottom)

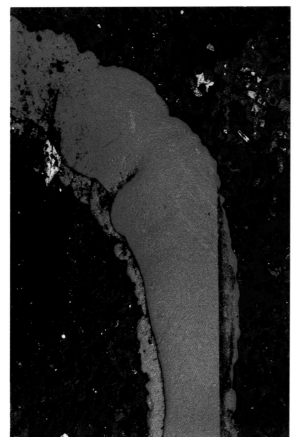 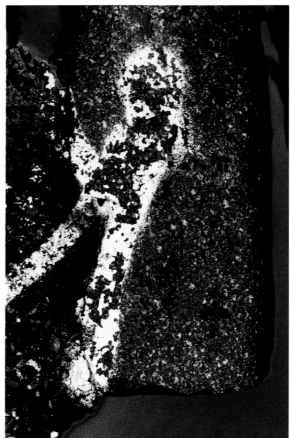

Photographer: SANDERS NICOLSON
Printer: Darren Hedges – Flash
Red Route

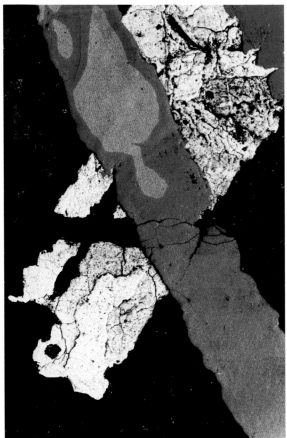

Photographer: SANDERS NICOLSON
Printer: Darren Hedges – Flash
Red Route

Great photography is the inspiration of our industry, and by furthering that aim we hope many aspiring newcomers will be encouraged to push their abilities further and discover the satisfaction of strong image making for themselves.

They can't do this unaided and the work in this book is a fine way of illustrating what is possible with a good eye and a sound idea.

Olympus have long been keen supporters of this philosophy with a regular and ongoing commitment to exhibitions, awards and individuals who further the same belief.

The Association of Photographers' Awards have always played a major part in such thinking and Olympus are delighted once more to contribute sponsorship to the 'Oscars' of photography.

IAN DICKENS

Communications Director

Olympus Cameras

Sponsored by

OLYMPUS
CAMERAS

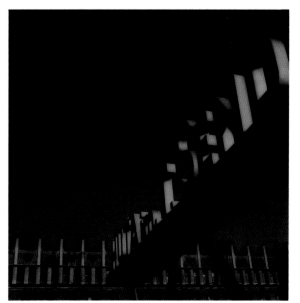 

SILVER

Photographer: AERNOUT OVERBEEKE
Printer: Aernout Overbeeke
Poland

Photographer: AERNOUT OVERBEEKE
Printer: Aernout Overbeeke
Poland

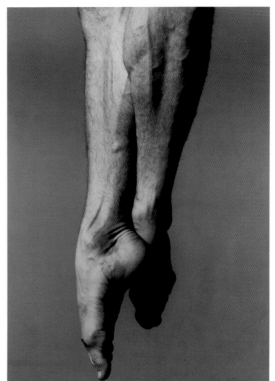

Photographer: JAMES WORMSER
Printer: Bill Rowlinson
Ballet Studies

MERIT

Photographer: JAMES WORMSER
Printer: Bill Rowlinson
Ballet Studies

Photographer: ALLAN McPHAIL
Printer: Tony White
Varmalid, Iceland
Leugarbakki, Iceland

Photographer: ALLAN McPHAIL
Printer: Tony White
Miklibaer, Iceland

Photographer: PETE SEAWARD
Printer: Daniel – Metro
Edvard, The Swiss Cowman

Photographer: PETE SEAWARD
Printer: Daniel – Metro
Edvard, The Swiss Cowman

Photographer: PETER HINCE
Printer: Klaus Kalde
The Maldives

Photographer: PETER HINCE
Printer: Klaus Kalde
The Maldives

COMMISSIONED ADVERTISING COLOUR

Colour photography is where 'Melinex' makes the difference, which is why I am very pleased to be able to sponsor this category of The Awards.

'Melinex' is a supergloss white polyester material from ICI. 'Melinex' is the alternative to resin coated paper and gives extra depth, improved definition and vibrant colours to your image. It lasts longer too – what more could the profession ask for?

PETER STAINER
Technical Manager Photo
Melinex from ICI Films

Sponsored by

Photographer: ALLAN McPHAIL
Printer Dan Tierney
Client: Nike
Commissioned by: Wieden & Kennedy – Amsterdam
Art Director: Robert Nakata

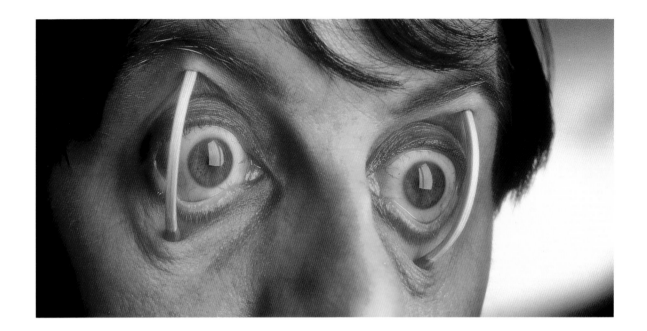

Photographer:	ROBERT WALKER
Printer:	Jason Moorhouse – Colour 061
Client:	Sealy Beds
Commissioned by:	Robson Brown
Art Director:	Duncan McEwan
Model:	John Last
Model Maker:	Peter Kidd – Invent

Photographer:	KENNETH GRIFFITHS
Client:	Speedo
Commissioned by:	Grey, London
Art Director:	Steve Jones
Creative Director:	Mike Elliott
Writer:	Martin Loraine
Art Buyer:	Angela Watkiss
Colour Retouchers:	Wace Creative Imaging

Photographer:	JONATHAN KNOWLES
Printer:	Mike Davis – Metro
Client:	Sony TV–Europe
Commissioned by:	Interfocus
Art Director:	Sarah MacKenzie

Photographer: ALLAN GRAINGER
Printer: Allan Grainger
Client: Hush Puppies
Commissioned by: Young & Rubicam
Art Director: Graeme Norways

ILFORD are delighted to again be sponsoring the Commissioned Advertising Black & White category of the Awards.

As one of the original sponsors of these awards it is encouraging to see how they have grown in prestige and popularity and that the black and white continues to be an important part of the competition.

ILFORD remains committed to the continued development of black and white products for the professional photographer, with our latest product Multigrade IV RC de luxe having many advantages over our previous Multigrade papers.

Our congratulations to all the winners of the Twelfth Awards.

BILL TIMMIS
Marketing and Planning Manager
Ilford

Sponsored by

Photographer: CHRIS FRAZER SMITH
Printer: Adrian Ensor
Client: Tampax
Commissioned by: The Design Works
Designer: Fiona Duck & Linda Manzi

Photographer: MATT HARRIS
Printer: Matt Harris
Client: Independent Perspective/Swale Housing
Commissioned by: Jeremy Woolwich (I.P.)
Art Director: Margarite Fischbach

Photographer: SEAMUS RYAN
Printer: Klaus Kalde
Client: The Sun
Commissioned by: Simons Palmer Denton Clemmow Johnson
Art Director: Guy Moore
Mr Bigwig

Photographer: CHRIS CHEETHAM
Printer: Peter – The Image
Client: Barclays Bank
Commissioned by: Warner Pini
Art Director: Chris Warner

Photographer: CHARLES DICKINS
Printer: Robin Bell
Client: NSPCC
Commissioned by: WWAV Rapp Collins
Art Director: Mike Eglington
Frightening Fred

The Awards of the Association of Photographers has now established itself as the most important creative benchmark and shop window of the industry.

Whilst the industry itself is reeling and adjusting to the rapid changes in technology, Primary Colour seeks to offer a strong reliable support for creativity in the manner a trellis offers purchase to a climbing rose. At this time we take care our trellis is neither painted too brightly nor casts a shadow causing us to lose sight of the beauty of the flower.

Through technical excellence and personal attention of our staff, Primary Colour is proud and committed to give unyielding support to photographers and their art.

BRIAN DE KRETZER
Primary Colour

sponsored by

Photographer: ANDREW SHAYLOR
Printer: Mike Davis – Metro
Client: Harmsworth Magazines
Commissioned by: Rebecca Hawtrey
Art Director: Rebecca Hawtrey
The Diver

Photographer: JOHN OFFENBACH
Printer: John Croggin
Client: The Inside
Art Directors: Cliff Lewis & Justin Nichols

For over 25 years, Dicomed Inc. has fostered the practical application of digital imaging and electronic retouching to the creative endeavours of professional photographers and retouchers worldwide.

From our introduction of the industry's first film recorders, imaging workstations and software, through our newest breakthroughs in high-resolution digital cameras, Dicomed has championed the alliance between the art of photography and the science of digital imaging.

In thanks to the many Members of The Association whose invaluable suggestions and creative contributions have helped us to design sophisticated imaging products, Dicomed is especially honoured to be sponsoring The Association of Photographers Twelfth Awards for the first time this year.

TREVOR HAWORTH

President & CEO

Dicomed inc.

Sponsored by

MERIT

Photographer: BARRY MARSDEN
Printer: Barry Marsden
Client: Daily Telegraph
Commissioned by: Sue Steward
Tony Curtis

Photographer:	TONY MAY
Printer:	Ron Bagley
Client:	Pink Floyd
Commissioned by:	Pink Floyd
Art Director:	Storm Thorgerson, M. Breedon, P. Curzon
Location:	Ely. Very cold in February
Model Maker:	Model Solutions

Photographer: JACQUI BISHOP WORNELL
Printer: Jacqui Bishop Wornell & Keith Taylor
Client: BIBIC
Commissioned by: BHP
Art Director: Keith Chapman

Photographer: DAVID TACK
Printer: Master Mono
Client: Cathay Pacific
Art Director: David Tack

Photographer: PETER SHERRARD
Printer: Peter Sherrard
Commissioned by: Polydor Records
Art Director: Jackie Fisher

Photographer: ROBERT WALKER
Printer: Mat Wright
Client: Creed
Commissioned by: Creed
Art Director: Robert Walker

Photographer:	TESSA TRAEGER
Printer:	Tony White
Client:	Festival des Arts, St Agrève
Commissioned by:	Paull Boucher
Art Director:	Patrick Kinmonth
	Mons. Paul Genest

Tapestry's continuing sponsorship of The Awards is founded on the belief that we are supporting the highest standards in creative and technical photography in the world. Standards that we always endeavour to reflect in Tapestry's service.

Many of our clients have achieved acclaim in previous Association Awards, so we trust that our reliability and quality have helped them to focus on their work, safe in the knowledge that they have dependable support from Tapestry.

We wish all Association members future success with their photographs and hope to see more of you in 1995.

Tapestry

Sponsored by

TAPESTRY

Photographer: BARRY LATEGAN
Client: Vodaphone
Commissioned by: Saatchi & Saatchi
Art Director: Bob Gabriel
System Operator: Hilary Brooks – Obscura

Photographer:	PAUL WAKEFIELD
Printer:	Quicksilver
Client:	1664 Kronenbourg
Commissioned by:	BDPP Paris
Art Director:	Damien Bellon
System Operator:	Actis

                 Photographer: PETER LAVERY
                      Printer: Tapestry
                       Client: Marlboro
               Commissioned by: Bainsfair Sharkey Trott
                 Art Director: Gordon Smith
               System Operator: Tapestry

Photographer:	ADRIAN BURKE
Client:	Perrier
Commissioned by:	Publicis
Art Director:	Rick Ward
System Operator:	Actis
Model Maker:	Gavin Lindsay
Background Painter:	David Bannister
Model:	Richard Oke
	Berrier

Since it was established in 1972, CETA Services Ltd. has gained a deserved reputation as one of the most forward-looking professional laboratory groups in London. The three laboratories making up CETA Services – the headquarters in Poland Street, W1, the location in St John Street, EC1 and the Kensington branch in Queensgate Mews, SW7 – each provide facilities encompassing every aspect of professional photo processing.

At its Poland Street headquarters, CETA has opened its Electronic Imaging Service Centre and it will be more, much more, than just another electronic imaging bureau, featuring the finest colour management system in the electronic imaging arena, the Dicomed Colour Advantage.

CETA is committed to continually improve its service to the point where the user – even the raw novice – can demystify the potentially confusing arena of electronic input and output. Hence the staffing of the bureau with proven experts in the field, familiar with every aspect of electronic imaging.

STEVE KENT

Managing Director

CETA Services Ltd

Sponsored by

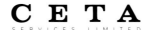

C E T A
SERVICES LIMITED

MERIT

Photographer: KEVIN GRIFFIN
Printer: Richard Jessup – Keishi Print
Client: Cable & Wireless
Commissioned by: Chiat Day
Art Director: David Buonaguidi
Sculptor: Jonathon Froud
The Line

Photographer:	KEVIN GRIFFIN
Printer:	Richard Jessup – Keishi Print
Client:	Cable & Wireless
Commissioned by:	Chiat Day
Art Director:	David Buonaguidi
Sculptor:	Jonathon Froud
	The Line

MERIT

Photographer: MALCOLM VENVILLE
Printer: Mike Davis – Metro
Client: NYNEX
Commissioned by: Chiat Day, New York
Art Director: Eric Houseknecht
Retouching: Tom Finnane – Wace
Casting: Mugshots

MERIT

Photographer: MALCOLM VENVILLE
Printer: Metro
Client: NYNEX
Commissioned by: Chiat Day, New York
Art Director: Eric Houseknecht
System Operator: Wace

Photographer: DAVID STEWART
Printer: Simon Bell
Client: Heals
Commissioned by: Leagas Shafron Davis Chick Ayer
Art Director: Mark Reddy

Photographer: DAVID STEWART
Printer: Simon Bell
Client: Heals
Commissioned by: Leagas Shafron Davis Chick Ayer
Art Director: Mark Reddy

Photographer: GRAHAM FORD
Printer: Richard Jessup
Client: Absolut Vodka
Commissioned by: TBWA, Paris
Art Director: Pascale Gayraud
Model Maker: Guy Hodgkinson
Absolut Paris, Absolut Vienna

Photographer:	GRAHAM FORD
Printer:	Richard Jessup
Client:	Absolut Vodka
Commissioned by:	TBWA, Paris
Art Director:	Pascale Gayraud
Model Maker:	Guy Hodgkinson
	Absolut Athens, Absolut Brussels

Photographer:	PETER LAVERY
Client:	Bacardi
Commissioned by:	McCann Erickson
Art Director:	John Scully
System Operator:	Lifeboat Matey

Photographer: PETER LAVERY
Client: Bacardi
Commissioned by: McCann Erickson
Art Director: John Scully
System Operator: Lifeboat Matey

Photographer:	BARRY LATEGAN
Printer:	Metro
Client:	Kenwood
Commissioned by:	Cowan Kemsley Taylor
Art Director:	Tim Johnson

Photographer:	BARRY LATEGAN
Printer:	Metro
Client:	Kenwood
Commissioned by:	Cowan Kemsley Taylor
Art Director:	Tim Johnson

K JP's parent company recently demonstrated its increasing support for, and commitment to, professional photography through its acquisition of the American group, Calumet Holdings Inc.

Our newly expanded organisation, the Calumet International Group, is 100% British owned and has become the world's largest distribution network for professional photographic equipment, materials and services, spanning the UK, USA and Western Europe.

Additionally, our manufacturing division now embraces world leading brands including Bowens, Cambo, Zone VI and Fidelity.

However, our success is not derived from getting bigger, but from getting better – spending more time talking to you, our customers, and finding more out about you, your work and your needs – and then doing our best to meet and exceed them.

To play a part in helping members of The Association of Photographers stay at the forefront of creative excellence is reward in itself – to sponsor the Twelfth Awards an added bonus.

STUART WALLACE

Group Marketing Director

KJP Ltd

part of the Calumet International Group

Sponsored by

SILVER

Photographer: MALCOLM VENVILLE
Client: FF Magazine
Commissioned by: Ogilvy & Mather, Frankfurt
Art Director: Dietmar Reinhard
Casting: Mugshots
Styling: Jane Field

SILVER

Photographer:	MALCOLM VENVILLE
Client:	FF Magazine
Commissioned by:	Ogilvy & Mather, Frankfurt
Art Director:	Dietmar Reinhard
Casting:	Mugshots
Styling:	Jane Field

SILVER

Photographer: PETER LAVERY
Printer: Tapestry
Client: Marlboro
Commissioned by: Bainsfair Sharkey Trott
Art Director: Gordon Smith
System Operator: Tapestry

SILVER

Photographer: PETER LAVERY
Printer: Tapestry
Client: Marlboro
Commissioned by: Bainsfair Sharkey Trott
Art Director: Gordon Smith
System Operator: Tapestry

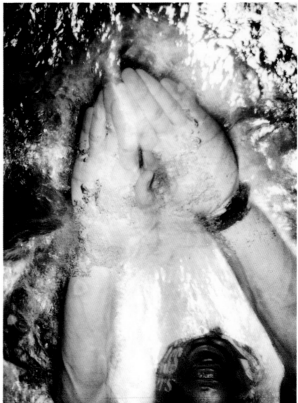

MERIT

Photographer: KELVIN MURRAY
Printer: Pete Guest – The Image
Commissioned by: S.C.S.C.

Photographer: KELVIN MURRAY
Printer: Pete Guest – The Image
Commissioned by: S.C.S.C.

MERIT

Photographer: TESSA TRAEGER
Printer: Tony White
Client: Festival des Arts, St Agrève
Commissioned by: Paull Boucher
Art Director: Patrick Kinmonth
Chestnut Harvest in the Ardèche

MERIT

Photographer: TESSA TRAEGER
Printer: Tony White
Client: Festival des Arts, St Agrève
Commissioned by: Paull Boucher
Art Director: Patrick Kinmonth
Chestnut Harvest in the Ardèche

Photographer: AERNOUT OVERBEEKE
Printer: Aernout Overbeeke
Client: Heineken
Commissioned by: PMSVW/Young & Rubicam
Art Director: Gerard van der Hart

Photographer:	AERNOUT OVERBEEKE
Printer:	Aernout Overbeeke
Client:	Heineken
Commissioned by:	PMSVW/Young & Rubicam
Art Director:	Gerard van der Hart

Photographer:	GINO SPRIO
Printer:	Gino Sprio
Client:	Empire Magazine
Commissioned by:	Roz Stevens
Art Director:	Stephen Fawcett
	Ismail Merchant, Film Director
	Jean-Jacques Beineix, Film Director

Photographer:	GINO SPRIO
Printer:	Gino Sprio
Client:	Empire Magazine
	ES Magazine (right)
Commissioned by:	Roz Stevens
	Wendy Hinton (right)
Art Director:	Stephen Fawcett
	John Turturro, Actor/Director
	Genevieve Jolliffe, Film Producer (right)

"Art is ruled uniquely by imagination. Images are its only wealth. It does not classify objects, it does not pronounce them real or imaginary, does not qualify them, does not define them; it feels and presents them – nothing more." Benedetto Croce (Esthetic, Ch 1)

The purpose of the Experimental category is to encourage and to recognise the artistic nature of photography. Polaroid materials are a photographer's aid to artistic interpretation. Thank you for supporting us.

CHARLIE YIANOULLOU
·European Marketing Manager
Professional Photography
Polaroid

Sponsored by

Photographer: MATTHEW ANTROBUS
Printer: Matthew Antrobus

Photographer: MICHAEL DUNNING
Printer: Mike Davis – Metro
Art Director: Michael Dunning

Photographer: STEVE BIELSCHOWSKY
Printer: Peter Trew – RT Printers
Lavinia at home

The Association Awards, now in their twelfth year, continue to flourish. Each year they provide us with an evocative exhibition of creative and technical excellence – original thought in a commercial world.

At Kodak we see ourselves as partners in this never ending quest for excellence. The depth of our professional product range is unrivalled in the marketplace – a Kodak application for every imaging situation.

We provide the tools. You do the rest.

CHRIS TOMBS

Director and General Manager

Kodak Professional Imaging and Printing Imaging

Sponsored by

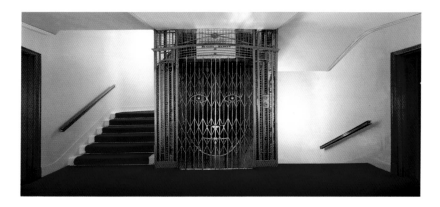

MERIT

Photographer: ANDREAS HEUMANN
Printer: Peter Young – Quicksilver (top)
Henrik Thorup Knudsen (bottom)
Client: Gallagher & Lyle (top)
Commissioned by: CDP (top)
Model Maker: Gavin Lindsay (top)
System Operator: Andreas Heumann (top)
Marina's hand in water (bottom)

MERIT

Photographer: ANDREAS HEUMANN
Printer: Andreas Heumann (left)
Andreas Heumann/Henrik Thorup Knudsen (right)
Sonam's Bindi, India (left)

MERIT

Photographer: ANDREAS HEUMANN
Printer: Andreas Heumann/Henrik Thorup Knudsen (top)
Andy Fisher – Ceta (bottom)
Commissioned by: Ceta (bottom)
Donkey in Ireland (top)

Photographer: ANDREAS HEUMANN
Printer: Andreas Heumann (top)
Peter Young – Quicksilver (bottom)
System Operator: Andreas Heumann (bottom)
White Cock, India (top)

MERIT

Photographer: MALCOLM VENVILLE
Printer: Mike Davis – Metro
Styling: Deborah Ferguson
Hair: Rocky
Make-up: Fiona Corrigan
Sascha Robertson

MERIT

Photographer: MALCOLM VENVILLE
Printer: Mike Davis – Metro
Costume: Jane Field
Hair & Make-up: Julie Dartnell
Set: Jeremy Pegg
Tarquin 'Incapability' Denton
His Reverence Pious Small Piece, Bishop of Chalfont St Giles
from a series of ancestral portraits of Mark Denton

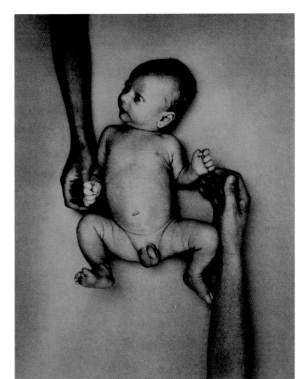

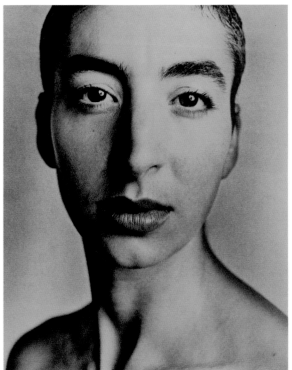

Photographer: MALCOLM VENVILLE
Printer: Mike Crawford – Lighthouse Darkroom
Oscar Robertson (left)
Edith Spiro (right)

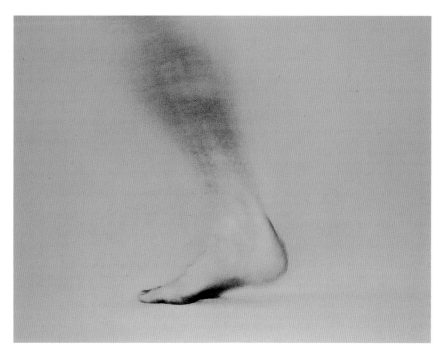

Photographer: MALCOLM VENVILLE
Printer: Mike Crawford – Lighthouse Darkroom
Client: Adidas
Commissioned by: Leagas Delaney
Art Director: Martin Galton
Martin Durban's foot (top) Runner (bottom)

"Whatever happened to the lovely shot of ...? I really liked that one and it didn't even make it into the second round."

This and similar comments are heard every year as the judges relax after the taxing job of reducing thousands of photographs to the final selection for the exhibition and book. It is, in fact, the very nature of competitions, that people will always disagree to some extent.

It is with this in mind that the Awards Committee has created this new special category called 'Judges' Choice'.

Each judge was asked if he or she wished to select a photograph from the huge pool of worthy 'also rans' and promote it into the book. This single image could have come from any category, including series and portfolios, the only stipulation being that it must come from otherwise unselected entries.

All but three of the judges this year have used this opportunity and we present these noteworthy outsiders on the following pages – each annotated with the name of the judge who rescued it from the cutting room floor.

With a considerable number of previous award winners now having their work represented through The Telegraph Colour Library, it is with great pleasure that this year we have taken the step to become the first stock library to support directly The Association Awards.

The range and quality of images available as stock has increased enormously in recent years. The Telegraph Colour Library has been at the forefront of this development and has a continuing commitment to representing photography of the highest quality. As a company our success is based on the power of the individual image. We therefore feel our sponsorship of the new Judges' Choice category to be particularly appropriate since this was also created to reward photographers for exceptional individual images.

TIM LUND
Director of Photography
Telegraph Colour Library

Sponsored by

Photographer: ANDREAS HEUMANN
Printer: Andy Fisher – Ceta
Client: Germany, BT
Commissioned by: Abbott Mead Vickers
Art Director: Andy Arghrou
System Operator: Andreas Heumann

Selected by Graham Henderson
from Commissioned Series Colour

Photographer: JONATHAN OAKES
Printer: Colour 061
Sailor

Selected by Aidan Sullivan
from Personal Life

Photographer: JONATHAN ROOT
Printer: Andrew Main
Foundry

Selected by Vince Frost
from Personal Life

Photographer: JONATHAN ROOT
Printer: Andrew Main
Ben & Craig

Selected by Gary Martin
from Personal Life

Photographer: PEER LINDGREEN
Printer: Peer Lindgreen

Selected by Tony Bowran
from Personal Life

Photographer: JAN CHLEBIK
Printer: Marshall Walker
34th Street, New York

Selected by Wendy Hinton
from Personal Series Black & White

Photographer: ALLAN GRAINGER
Printer: Allan Grainger
Client: Alliance & Leicester
Commissioned by: BMP DDB Needham
Art Director: Peter Gatley & Tony Davidson

Selected by Peter Myers
from Commissioned Advertising Black & White

Photographer: DUNCAN McNICOL
Printer: Bill Rowlinson
Bar, Milly La Forêt

Selected by David Pearce
from Personal Landscape/Sense of Place

Photographer: JAMES WORMSER
Printer: Phil Holding – Push One
Kipper Antithesis

Selected by Mark Reddy
from Personal Still Life

Photographer: ANDREAS HEUMANN
Printer: Jean Lock – Visions
Tricycle Break, India

Selected by Tim Motion
from Personal Landscape/Sense of Place

Photographer: AERNOUT OVERBEEKE
Printer: Aernout Overbeeke
Spain

Selected by Tom Stoddart
from Portfolio

Photographer:	TIM FLACH
Printer:	Bill Rowlinson
Animal Handler:	Jim Clubb
	Atlas the Lion

Selected by Ray Massey
from Personal Life

Photographer: HENRIK THORUP KNUDSEN
Printer: Carlos Olalla – Ceta
Ring Side

Selected by Martin Galton
from Personal Life

Photographer:	DEAN STEADMAN
Printer:	John – Direct Colour
Client:	Johnny Walker Red Label
Commissioned by:	WCRS
Art Director:	Rooney Carruthers

Selected by Mick Dean
from Commissioned Advertising Colour

The bulk of our membership are professional photographers, working in our three specialist areas – fashion, advertising and editorial. The balance is made up of assistants, agents, colleges and the industries leading companies. We have recently introduced a new category for the discerning "Friend".

By joining The Association of Photographers you become part of the most influential photographic organisation in the UK. You can be involved at an early stage with the professional and practical challenges that lie ahead and participate in new ideas and initiatives to help determine a positive and exciting future.

For an information pack or membership details please contact Janice Nemitz, The Membership Secretary at The Association of Photographers, 9-10 Domingo Street, London EC1Y OTA. Telephone 0171-608 1441.

Aart Aan de Weil
James Abelson
Geoff Adams
Lorenzo Agius
Deyana Ahmadi
Stak Aivaliotis
Daniel Allan
Christopher Ambrose
Matthew Antrobus
John Aparicio
Peter Aprahamian
Miguel Arana
Caroline Arber
Jim Arnould
Chris Arthur
Sue Atkinson
Kevin J Attfield
Bryce Attwell

Chris Bailey
Dequincey Bailey
Susan Baker
Tom Baker
Jan Baldwin
Ron Bambridge
Bryan Bane
Jack Bankhead
Michael Banks
Zafer Baran
Edward Barber
Robert Barber
Christopher Barker
Colin Barker
John Barlow
Matthew Barlow
Martin Barraud
Peter Barry
Neil Barstow
Andy Barter
Greg Bartley
Karl Bartley
Ian Batchelor
Jennifer Bates
Simon Battensby
Peter Beavis
Martin Beckett
Jean-Luc Benard
Oliver Benn

Geoffrey Benson
Adri Berger
Bert Berghuis
Theo Bergstrom
Derek Berwin
Paul Bevitt
Paul Biddle
Steve Bielschowksy
Berry Bingel
Peter Birch
Malcolm Birkett
Jacqui Bishop
John Bishop
Martin Black
Michael Black
Anthony Blake
Patrick Blake
Chris Bland
John Blomfield
Christopher Booth
Tim Booth
Harry Borden
Mike Botha
Roy Botterell
Clive Boursnell
Tony Bowran
Padraig Boyle
Adrian Bradbury
Richard Bradbury
Stephen Bradley
Larry Bray
Geoff Brightling
John T Brightmore
Rob Brimson
Robin Broadbent
Michael Brockway
Alan Brooking
Martyn J Brooks
Bruce Brown
Heather Brown
John Brown
Simon Brown
Gary Bryan
Alex Buckingham
Barry Bullough
Gerrit Buntrock
David Burch
Hugh Burden

Marc Burden
Desmond Burdon
Roger J Burge
Adrian Burke
Alexandra Burke
Dan Burn-Forti
Paul Bussell

Julian Calder
Michael Caldwell
Julian Calverley
Andrew Cameron
Tommy Candler
Nick Carman
Rory Carnegie
Wendy Carrig
Paul Carroll
David Cartledge
Ian D Cartwright
Lorna Cattell
Steve Cavalier
Phil Cawley
Jean Cazals
Sandra Cecil
Martin Chaffer
David Chambers
Chris Cheetham
Don Chesser
Jane Chilvers
Pete Chinn
Jan Chlebik
Stuart Chorley
Ken Christie
Philip Chudy
John Clamp
John Claridge
Richard Clark
Michael Clement
Niall Clutton
Alwyn R Coates
Patrick Cocklin
David Cockroft
Tessa Codrington
Stephen Coe
Stephanie Colasanti
John Cole
Andy Collison
Stephen Colover

Bryn Colton
Stuart Colwill
Tim Cook
Angela Coombes
Graeme Cooper
Rick Cordell
Tobi Corney
James Cotier
Gavin Cottrell
John Couzins
Christopher Cowan
Roger Cracknell
Bob Cramp
John Crane
Chris Craymer
Alun Crockford
Harriet Cullen
Lupe Cunha
Doug Currie
Kathy Curshen
William G Curtis
Will Curwen
Colin Cuthbert

Lou D'Angelo
Ian Dagnall
Nick Daly
Robert Daly
Jack Daniels
Geoffrey Dann
Keith Davies
Duncan Davis
Mark Davison
Peter Dazeley
Julian de Havilland
Victor De Schwanberg
Mick Dean
Julian Deghy
Antonia Deutsch
Charles Dickins
Julie Dixon
Michael Dmochowski
Cliff Dodd
Stephen Dodd
Nick Dolding
Terence Donovan
William Douglas
Philip Dowell

Robert Dowling
David Downie
Chris Dreja
Tim Dry
Michael Duff
Michael Dunning
Dale Durfee
Michael Dyer

Julian Easten
Roger Eaton
Jillian Edelstein
Ben Edwards
Andreas Einsiedel
Clint Eley
Mike Ellis
Robert Elsdale
Robert Enever
Dilwyn Evans
Koren Evans
Laurie Evans
Frances Evelegh
Martin Evening

David Fairman
Simon Farnhell
Richard Faulks
Katherine Fawssett
John Fenton
Frank Fernandez
Nick Ferrand
John Ferrara
Des Fildes
Graham Finlayson
Conrad Fisher
Julie Fisher
Tim Flach
Paul Flanagan
Adrian Flowers
Mark Follon
Colin Ford
Graham Ford
Max Forsythe
Wayne Forward
Paul M Fosbury
Arthur Foster
Geoff Franklin
Don Fraser

Ian Fraser
Christopher Frazer-Smith
John Freebrey
Geoffrey Frosh
Clive Frost
Trevor Fulford
Bob Fyffe

Kate Gadsby
Ray Gaffney
Christopher Gale
Andy Gallacher
David Gamble
David Garcia
Glen Garner
Mark M Gaskin
Mark Gatehouse
Paul Gates
Gerry Gavigan
Nick Georghiou
Tracey Gibbs
Tony Gilbert
David Gill
Colin Glanfield
Richard Glover
Rolph Gobits
Tim Goffe
Tina Golden
Mike Goss
James Graham
Allan Grainger
Karl Grant
Tom Graty
Stephen Gray
Andy Green
David Greenwood
Kevin Griffin
Kenneth Griffiths
Guy Grundy
Lorentz Gullachsen
Andrew Gulland
Tim Gummer
David Guyon

Bill Halford
Andrew Hall
David Hall
Jon Hall

Stuart Hamilton
Keith Hammond
Alan Hampson
Christine Hanscomb
Michael Harding
Bob Harris
Gina Harris
Graeme Harris
Matt Harris
Tony Harris
Mark Harrison
Mark Harwood
Laurie Haskell
Martin Haswell
Jason Hawkes
Laurie Haynes
Nigel Haynes
Tim Hazael
Elisabeth Henderson
Graham Henderson
Frank Herholdt
Herbert Herzl
John Heseltine
Andreas Heumann
Amanda Heywood
John Higginson
Shaun P Higson
Ferguson Hill
John Hill
Martin Hill
Tim Hill
Hans Hiltermann
Jane Hilton
Peter Hince
Adam Hinton
Bay Hippisley
Graham Hitchcock
Andrew G Hobbs
Philip Holden
Anthony Holmes
Marty Holt
Martin Hooper
Ian Hooton
Tony Hopewell
Charles Hopkinson
Michael Hoppen
Christopher Hopper
Ed Horwich

Steve Hoskins
Kelvin Hudson
Neil Hudson
Alistair Hughes
Jamie Hughes
Malcolm Hulme
Tim Hunt
Tif Hunter
Tony Hutchings

Janet Ibbotson
Tim Imrie
Rowan Isaac

Phil Jason
Lu Jeffery
Robert Jobling
Amanda Jobson
Hugh Johnson
Keith Johnson
Allan Jones
Hywel Jones
Michael Joseph
Branka Jukic
Mark Junak

Ian Kalinowski
David Kampfner
Nadav Kander
Judith Katz
George Kavanagh
Michael Kay
Ashton Keiditsch
David Kelly
Howard Kemp
Jhon Kevern
Gavin Kingcome
Andrew Kingsbury
Howard Kingsnorth
Ken Kirkwood
Jutta Klee
Peter Knab
John Knill
Karen Knorr
Jonathan Knowles
Tony Knuff
Bob Komar
Jess Koppel

Markku Lahdesmaki
Alistair Laidlaw
Peter Lake
Bob Lambert
Geoff Langan
Mark Lanning
Sue Lanzon
Simon Larbalestier
Barry Lategan
Tony Latham
Heinz Lautenbacher
Peter Lavery
Mark Lawrence
John Lawrence Jones
Mike Laye
Simon Lee
Stephen Lee
Martin Leeks
Brian Leonard
Eleni Leoussi
Chris Lewis
Di Lewis
Patrick Lichfield
John E Linden
Jon Lippett
Martin Lipscombe
Peter Littlewood
George Logan
Derek Lomas
John Londei
Pauline Lord
Sandra Lousada
Jonathan Lovekin
Cornel Lucas
Jacqueline Lucas Palmer
Ron Lucking
Grantly S Lynch
Marcus Lyon
Carl Lyttle

John Mac
Neil MacKenzie Matthews
Bruce A Mackie
Niall Macleod
Tim MacPherson
Tom Main
Tim Malyon
Eric Mandel

Barry Marsden
Alan Marsh
Anthony Marsland
John Mason
Mark Mason
Ray Massey
Kiran Master
Robert Masters
Kit Constable Maxwell
Marcia May
Matthew May
Tony May
Linda McCartney
Fi McGhee
Michael McGoran
Iain McKell
Ian McKinnell
Kirsty McLaren
James McMillan
Duncan McNicol
Allan McPhail
Ralph Medland
Nick Meers
Paul Mellor
Neill Menneer
James Merrell
James Meyer
Axel Michel
Mark Middlebrook
John Midgley
Bob Miller
Diana Miller
Glenn Millington
Allan Mills
Colin Mills
Paul Mitchell
Moggy
Colin Molyneux
Graeme Montgomery
David Moore
Vernon Morgan
Adamo Morgese
Stephen Morley
Christopher Morris
Greg Morris
Leon Morris
Sara Morris
Ralph Mortimer

Bill Morton
John Moss
Tim Motion
Sam Moxon
Chris Moyse
Lewis Mulatero
Tom Mulvee
James Murphy
Paul Murphy
Kelvin Murray
Allan Mushen
Peter Myers
Jay Myrdal

Horst Neumann
Steve Newman
Alan Newnham
Patrick Nicholas
George Nicholls
Sanders Nicolson
Julian Nieman
David Noton
Taly Noy

Ian O'Leary
Tim O'Sullivan
Mike O'Toole
Jonathan Oakes
Jerry Oke
Anthony Oliver
David Oliver
Andrew Olney
Lizzie Orme
Gill Orsman
Tony Othen
Aernout Overbeeke
Chris Overton
Mike Owen

Tony Page
Simon Page-Ritchie
Daniel Pangbourne
David Parfitt
Van Pariser
Clare Park
John Parker
Sue Parker
David Parmiter

Nigel Parry
Mike A Parsons
Colin Peacock
Robert Pedersen
Glen Percival
Glen Perotte
Kevin Peschke
Sergio Petrelli
Nick Philbedge
Carl S. Pinnington
Stephen Piotrowski
Tim Platt
Thomas I Pollock
Mark Polyblank
Russell Porcas
Sandy Porter
Fiona Pragoff
Richard Prescott
David Preutz
Nick Price
Susanna Price
Colin Prior
Ed Pritchard
Michael Pugh
Richard Pullar
Joshua Pulman
Justin Pumfrey
Con Putbrace

Ashton Radcliffe
Na'im A Rahman
Rodney Rascona
Peter Rauter
John Rawlings
Mark Rayner
Stuart Redler
Rocco J Redondo
Darran Rees
Paul Rees
Steve Rees
Antonia Reeve
Mike Reeves
Jeremy Rendell
Ben Rice
Ted Rice
Derek Richards
Trevor Richards
Bill Richmond

Eric Richmond
Tim Ridley
Martin Riedl
Nicholas Rigg
Andrew Roberts
Nick Roberts
Malcolm Robertson
Jeff Robins
Neil Robinson
Peter Robinson
Peter Rodger
Jonathan Root
Sarah Root
Taffi Rosen
John Ross
Joe Roughan
Dominic Rouse
Deborah Rowe
Jerome Le Roy-Lewis
David Rudkin
Stephanie Rushton
David Russell
Erik Russell
Mike Russell
Chris Ryan
Seamus Ryan

Russell Sadur
Derek Scarbrough
David Scheinmann
Herb Schmitz
Derek Seagrim
Derek Seaward
Peter Seaward
David Seed
Claus Semmler
Geoff Senior
Charles Settrington
Andy Seymour
Carol Sharp
John Shaw
Mike St Maur Sheil
Jason Shenai
Peter Sherrard
Rod Shone
David Short
Richard Sibley
Duncan Sim

Paul Simcock
Tim Simmons
Chris Simpson
John Sims
Tony Skinner
Michael Smallcombe
Duncan Smith
Geoff Smith
Grant Smith
Mike Smith
Peter Smith
Peter J Smith
Simon Smith
Andrew Snaith
George E Solomonides
Simon Somerville
John Spragg
Brian P Spranklen
Gino Sprio
Jeff Starley
Philip Starling
Dean Steadman
Charlie Stebbings
Moritz Steiger
Lars Stenman
Mark Stenning
Dan Stevens
Garry Stevenson
David Stewart
James Stewart
Jon Stewart
Dennis Stone
Peter Story
Anthony Straeger
Kevin Summers
Richard Surman
David Swan
Mike Swartz
Lucinda Symons

David Tack
Cymon Taylor
Nigel Taylor
Sara Taylor
Calvey Taylor-Haw
Steve Teague
Luca Invernizzi Tettoni
Han Chew Tham

Andrew J. Thomas
Colin Thomas
Peter Thompson
Steve Thompson
Stephen R Thornton
Peter Thorpe
Mark Tillie
John Timbers
David Tolley
Tessa Traeger
Jonathan Trapman
Debi Treloar
Terry Trott
Pia Tryde Sandeman
Nick Turley
Adrian Turner
Corinne Turner
John Turner
Robert Turner
Leslie Turtle
Adam Tysoe

David Usill

Mike Valente
Martin Vallis
Rohan Van Twest
Olaf Veltman
Mike Venables
Malcolm Venville
Stephen Vernon-Clarke
Patrice de Villiers
Manfred Vogelsanger

Richard Waite
Paul Wakefield
Roy Wales
Robert Walker
Andrew B Wallis
John Walmsley
David Walter
Huw Walters
Matthew Ward
Anthony Waring
Carl Warner
Malkolm Warrington
Ray Watkins
Denis Waugh

Uli Weber
Colin Thomas
Paul Webster
Matthew Weinreb
Rosemary Weller
Kenneth Wells
Paul Wenham-Clarke
Philip West
Graham Westmoreland
Andy Whale
Simon Wheeler
Tim White
Andrew Whittuck
Zanna Wilford
Reg Wilkins
Dai Williams
Glyn Williams
Michael Williams
Moy Williams
Peter Williams
Richard Williams
Justin Windle
Chris Windsor
Paul Windsor
Tim Windsor
Martin Wonnacott
Peter Wood
Simon Wood
Stuart Wood
Geoff Woods
Martin Woods
Adam Woolfitt
Ian Woollams
Jimmy Wormser
Andrew Wornell
Michael Wray
George Wright
James Bissett Wright
Adrian Wroth
Jon Wyand

Graham Young

Jacek Jan Zaluski
Elizabeth Zeschin

ASSISTANT MEMBERS
Lindsy Agana
Tim Ainsworth

Ian Aitken
Mark Alcock
Jane Alexander
John Alflatt
Mel Allen
Jonathan Andrew
Andy Andrews
Richard Apperly
Jose Aragon
Robert Ashton

James Barlow
Nicholas Barnard
Samuel Barton
Loz Baylis
Dean Belcher
Steve J. Benbow
Phillip Berryman
Paul Blackshaw
Paul Blinston
Ian Boddy
Paul Born
Enda Bowe
Mike Boyle
James Braund
Martin Breschinski
Adrian Brown
James Bunch
Simon Burch
David Burgess
Gavin Burke
Lesley Burke
Adrian Burt

Stuart Cain
Steve Callaghan
Sharon Cavanagh
Barry Cawston
Ian Chamberlain
Nigel Charman
Oswald Cheung
Nicholas Clark
Jim Colley
Adrian Cook
Ken Copsey
Richard Cornwall
Pamela Cowan
John Cumming

Stephen Dagger
Nick David
Nigel Davies
Neil Davis
Adam Dawe
Gemma Day
Peter Day
Grant Delin
Suki Dhanda
Christine Donnier-Valentin
Claudia Dulak
Russell Duncan
Gavin Durrant

Andy Eaves
Frea Eden
Raymond Ellis

Michael Fair
Douglas Falby
John Falzon
Guy Farrow
Gill Faulkner
Charlie Fawell
Robin Feild
Lucy Fitter
Indira Flack
Marty Forsyth
Eugenio Franchi
Julia Fullerton-Batten

Trish Gant
David Gargon
Caroline Garside
Joanne Gartside
Paul Gill
Andrew Glass
Victoria Gomez
Christopher Gonta
Michael Gough
Juliet Greene
Andrew Greig
Kostas Grivas

Stuart Hall
Jeremy Hardie
Nigel Harniman

Nicholas Harper
Michael Harvey
Philip Harvey
Sarah Harvey
Karen Hatch
Tim Hawkings
Lizzy Hearne
Luke Hickman
Jeremy Hilder
Anthony Hill
Robert Holmes
Jeremy Hopley
Colin Hoskins
Philip Howling
Graham Hughes
Phil Hunt

Neal Jackson
Nigel James
Annie Johnston

Eddie Kay
John Kelly
Liam Kennedy
Glenn Kenworthy
Andy Knight Ltd
Henrik Thorup Knudsen
Andrew Kruczek
Dana Kurlansky
Simon Kynaston
Tas Kyprianou
Artemi Kyriacou

Lea Laboure
Sandra Lambell
Steffen Landua
Chris Lawrenson
Neil Lawson
Dennis Lee
Shaky Lee
Simon Lefevre
Murray Lenton
Peer Lindgreen
Timothy Lofthouse
Tony Lumb
Paul Lund

Stuart MacGregor

Jeremy Maher
Theresa Maloney
James Marsden
Suzanne Marshall
Christian McGowan
Colin McKay
Paul McNicholas
Simon Mills
Caroline Molloy
Franco Monti
Gareth Morgan
Martin Morrell
Andy Morris
Trish Morrissey
Gareth Munden
Antonio Munoz
Deborah Murray
James Murray

Richard Neall
Mark Newbold
Stephen Nicholls

David Obadiah
John Offenbach
Fleur Olby
Chris Parker
Sue Parkhill
Louisa Parry
Susan Passmore
Paolo Patrizi
Craig Paulson
Jonathan Pegler
Bridget Peirson
Andrew Pendlebury
Martin Peters
Nigel Phillips
Marcus Pietrek
Philip Pinchin
Kate Plumb
Robert Pogson
Toby Pond
Sarah-Vivien Prescott
Sloane Pringle
Lucinda Pryor
Mark Purdom

Sarah Ramsay

Peter Reeves
Colin Renwick
Giles Revell
Marcel Reyes-Cortez
John Ridley
Stephen Rodgers
Kevin Roseblade
Stephen Rosewell
Keith Roughton
Kevin Rowley
Darrell Russell

Debbie Sandersley
Derrick Santini
John Savage
Rex Scroggie
Dennis Seed
Andrew Shaylor
Andrew Shennan
Hilary Slater
Andrew Southon
Leon Steele
Simon Stock
Michael Swallow
Adrian Swift

George Tappeiner
Mark Tasker
Gary Taylor
Stephen Thomas
Alan Thornton
Peter Tizzard
Jason Tozer
Charles Troman
Mark Turnbull
Malcolm Tute
Rob Van Der Vet
Ariel Van Straten
Ras Verdi

Cameron Watt
Everton Waugh
Mathew Webb
Joss Whittaker
John Glyn Williams
Barry Willis

Dave Willis

Tony Wong
Ben Wood
Mark Wood
Matthew Wright

James Yalden
Steve Yeates

AFFILIATED COMPANIES
Ceta Ltd
CID Publishing
Fuji Professional
Hasselblad UK Ltd
Joe's Basement
Keith Johnson + Pelling Ltd
Kodak Ltd
Nikon UK Ltd
Olympus Cameras
Polaroid UK Ltd

SUPPORTIVE MEMBERS
Sue Allatt
Peter Bailey
Richard Baynes
Sally Byron-Johnson
Mark Cumming
David Gardiner
Ziggy Golding
Susan Griggs
Madeleine Hamel
Niall Horton-Stephens
Jonathan Mallory
Jonathan Marsland
Steve Mayes
Pim Milo
Liz Moore
Charles Saddington
Tony Stone
Robert Toay
Laura Watts

FRIENDS OF THE ASSOCIATION
Bel January
Jonathan Topps

AFFILIATED COLLEGES
Barking College
Berkshire College of Art & Design
Blackpool & the Fylde College
Bournemouth & Poole College of Art & Design
Cheltenham & Gloucester College of Higher Education
City of Westminster College
Cleveland College of Art & Design
Dewsbury College
Falmouth College of Arts
Glasgow College Of Building & Printing
Glasgow School of Art
Kent Institute of Art & Design
Kingston Polytechnic
Napier University
Newcastle College
Norfolk College of Arts & Technology
Plymouth College of Art & Design
Salisbury College
Southampton Institute of Higher Education
Staffordshire University

If you are unable to contact any of these photographers on the telephone numbers listed please call The Association of Photographers on 0171-608 1441.

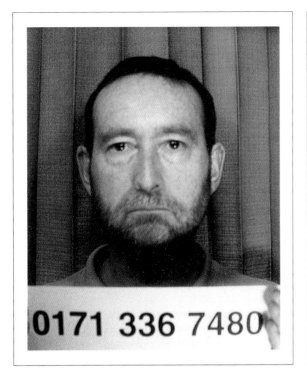
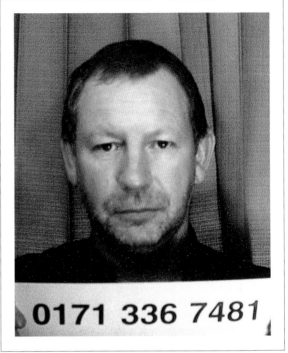

MERIT

Company:	SAWARD ROBERTS
Printer:	Photo booth at Barbican Station
Commissioned by:	The Association of Photographers
Address:	Northburgh House, 10 Northburgh Street
City:	London, EC1V 0AY
Telephone:	0171 336 7480/1
Facsimile:	0171 336 7481
Functions:	Design/Conventional & Digital Artwork/
	Typesetting/Brochures/Annual Reports/
	Advertisements/Books...

"At last a camera that can cope with whatever you throw at it."

"Let's be clear about this, the vast majority of the rich and famous love me taking their photograph.

But over the years, I have had the occasional show of reluctance.

I've had drink, food, even the odd punch thrown at me.

And while I can usually mop myself down or patch myself up, I can't always do the same for my cameras.

So I was intrigued when Olympus asked me to try their £99, weatherproof AF-1 Mini.

After all, if it could last a couple of nights on the town with me, a fortnight on the beach or the ski slopes wouldn't trouble it.

I can report that when things got stormy the AF-1 Mini coped remarkably.

It's as impervious to a drizzly night outside a club or a restaurant as it is to an accurately aimed glass of bubbly.

A sliding cover – clever, this – acts as an on/off switch and kept the lens clean and dry even when I chucked it in the pocket of my motorcycle jacket.

The fully automatic flash gives out 19 tiny pre-flashes before the main one, to help the dreaded "red-eye"– even in some of our more veteran rock stars.

Throw in automatic focus, film loading, advance and rewind and you've got yourself a very neat little package.

I think I might just hang onto one. Ivana's back in town."

OLYMPUS AF-1 Mini

You always see our name on most
of the pages in this book.

But this is the only one we've
ever actually paid for.

TAPESTRY 51-52 FRITH STREET, SOHO LONDON W1V 5TE.
TELEPHONE 071-287 3322 iSDN 071-734 5478 FAX 071-437 5713

Workstation: Dicomed Imaginator™ Pentia Pro
Photo-Imagination: Andrew Thomas

For more information, contact Dicomed at 01344 300 011 or Andrew Thomas, at 01753 790911

The Creative Handbook
Fax +44 (0) 1342 335948

(the key)

get out more OF *T*EN

THE
CREATIVE
HAND
BOOK
1995

designed by design narrative   images by emma parker

Trans **optic**

£2000 RETOUCHING

THERE ARE MANY JOBS, TODAY, THAT REQUIRE THE CAPABILITY, CAPACITY AND RESOLUTION OF COMPUTER-SYSTEM RETOUCHING. THERE ARE MANY RE-TOUCHING SYSTEMS RUN BY OPERATORS. THERE IS ONE SYSTEM THAT IS RUN WITH THE TRADITIONAL SKILLS, KNOW-HOW AND UNDERSTANDING OF THE HAND-RETOUCHER.

£600 RETOUCHING

THERE ARE STILL MANY JOBS, TODAY, THAT DO NOT NEED TO BE DONE ON SYSTEM, BUT SUFFER THE HIGH PRICE FOR WANT OF AN ALTERNATIVE. THERE IS A COMPANY THAT STILL OFFERS THE TRADITIONAL, QUICK AND LARGELY COST-EFFECTIVE SKILLS OF THE BEST HAND-RETOUCHERS FOR OUTSTANDING RESULTS THAT RESPECT THE BUGETRY CONSTRAINTS THAT WE ALL HAVE TO WORK UNDER AT ONE TIME OR ANOTHER.

Trans **colour**

Unit I, 7 Tyers Gate, Off Bermondsey St., London Bridge. SEI 3HX. Tel. 0171 403 0048, Fax 0171 403 1944